101 American English Riddles

Understanding Language and Culture Through Humor

Harry Collis

Illustrated by Joe Kohl

D1051200

Printed on recyclable paper

 **PASSPORT BOOKS**
a division of *NTC Publishing Group*
Lincolnwood, Illinois USA

Acknowledgments

I should like to express my appreciation to my colleague Alfredo Jordan for his inspired suggestions in envisioning the art for this book.

I am particularly grateful to my editor, Lynn M. Stafford, for providing the incisive direction and guidance that made possible the realization of this project.

Contents

Foreword

In learning a language, people reach a point where they are comfortable enough to start using word games, puns, double entendres, and even idioms in joking. Such word games are often used in short puzzles called *riddles*. Riddles are a luxury in any language, as they are used solely to entertain and engage one's listeners. For this reason, they fall outside the flow of normal conversation. Instead, they stand as independent, humorous bits of banter. One interesting feature of riddles is that they appeal to all age groups, from the wise-and-experienced to the very young.

Riddles go back to ancient times. Originally, they were posed to generate introspection and to teach lessons. They were used as part of sacred rituals, prophecies, and even matters of life and death. One of the most ancient riddles that has come down to us is the riddle of the Sphinx. The Sphinx, a mythological creature, stood guard over the gates of the city of Thebes and asked the following riddle of all who passed: "What walks on four legs in the morning, two legs at noon, and three legs at night?" Those who could not answer the riddle were killed. One day, a man named Oedipus solved the riddle and destroyed the Sphinx. He correctly interpreted "the morning" as infancy, when we crawl on our hands and knees. "Noon" represents the period of life when we walk on two feet as adults. "Night" refers to our old age, when we must use canes to walk.

Over the years, the nature of riddles has changed. Today in America, riddles are used to mislead, trick, and amuse. They have become a staple of American humor. As a linguistic puzzle, a riddle can be a test of one's cleverness or a way to challenge one's wits. Solving the riddle is as much a part of the fun as asking the riddle.

In *101 American English Riddles*, the solutions and the humor to many of the riddles come from the language itself.

English in particular has many words with more than one meaning. Consequently, these words constitute a vast storehouse of material from which a riddle may originate; for example: "How can a leopard change his spots?" Answer: "Move from place to place." The word *spot* can mean a "mark or stain," like the black spots on the coat of a leopard. It can also mean a "particular physical location."

101 American English Riddles include many types of language-based humor. The humor in some riddles lies in knowing the meaning of an idiomatic expression. Some riddles have words that sound alike, but have different spellings and, consequently, different meanings. Others are worded to focus your attention on a certain part of the question, all in an effort to confuse you. All of these riddles stimulate thought about language and are enjoyable learning tools for nonnative speakers of English.

However, not all riddles depend entirely on word play for their humor. In one of the most common types of riddle, the expected or logical solution turns out to be the wrong answer. For example, to the question "Why do surgeons wear masks during an operation?" one would expect an answer such as, "For sanitary purposes." However, the answer is, "So that if they make a mistake, no one will know who did it." The surprise ending of the riddle makes it funny.

101 American English Riddles has nine sections. Each section contains riddles that all rely on one type of language game or logic for their humor. The title of each section hints at the nature of the riddles to follow. Each riddle is accompanied by an illustration that exaggerates the humor of the riddle by focusing on its literal meaning or that hints at its solution.

Those riddles that contain particularly advanced language or grammar are followed by an explanatory note or dialogue that presents the language item in normal usage, exposing the student to natural American language samples. Many of the examples also contain contemporary expressions and idioms that will help to further develop the nonnative speaker's understanding of American English.

101 American English Riddles is a fun way to enjoy English and to learn it at the same time. Because of the quirky humor and illustrations, native speakers of English can also laugh at the riddles, though many will already be familiar.

Take your time with these riddles. Look at the clues that point toward the solution, and see if you can arrive at the answer on your own. Here's one to start with:

In the beginning, I seem mysterious, but in the end I'm nothing serious. What am I?

A riddle!

Section One

You Can't Have One Without the Other

These riddles contain compound words. These are words that combine two or more words into a single unit. To solve the riddles, you have to distinguish the meanings of the compound words from the meanings of their separate parts.

1   **What is a doughnut?**

Someone who is crazy about money.

A **doughnut** is a fried cake shaped like a ring. In slang, **dough** also means "money," and **nut** can mean "a crazy or eccentric person." If you are a **nut for something,** it means that you are extremely enthusiastic about it.

A: Richard, you're looking well. How about getting some coffee with me?

B: Coffee and doughnuts sounds great! So, what have you been up to lately? I haven't seen you for awhile.

A: Actually, I've been working around the clock in my new business.

B: Oh, you're after the big bucks, huh? I never thought you'd be so dedicated to money! You're becoming a real "dough nut"!

A: Yeah, and a health nut, too. I don't eat doughnuts anymore—they have too much fat!

2 What kind of pool can't you swim in?

A car pool.

A **pool** is a small body of water. It can also refer to a common supply of something, such as money, that can be used by a number of people. For example, when people drive together in the same car to save gas and money, it's called a **car pool.**

John and Brittany, along with several of their school friends, were invited for a swim at the Garcias' pool. The Garcias' house was far away and the kids wanted to drive together to save gas. They went in two car pools and spent the whole afternoon swimming.

3 How do you make an eggroll?

Push it.

An **eggroll** is a Chinese food made of dough wrapped around vegetables, egg, herbs, and spices. Of course, an **egg** is also a food itself. To **roll** is to move something by turning it round and round.

September 22 at Twain Elementary School is the Sixth Annual International Fun and Games Day. There will be games like the wheelbarrow race and the egg rolling contest. We'll also have international foods, including crepes, borscht, and eggrolls.

4 What suit lasts longer than you do?

A lawsuit.

A **suit** is a set of matching clothes that are worn together, especially for business wear. A **lawsuit** is an action taken in a court to secure justice.

Mr. Kim was worried. Today he had to appear in court because a lawsuit was being brought against him. Of course, he dressed up in his best suit for the trial so that he would look nice for the judge and jury.

5 Why did the little boy throw the butter out the window?

To see the butterfly.

Butter is a food product made from cream. **To fly** means to move through the air. (A **fly** is an ugly insect that can do this.) A **butterfly,** though, is a beautiful insect with brightly colored wings.

A: Jay, what are you doing with that stick of butter?

B: I'm going to throw it out the window. I want to see the butter fly.

A: Don't be silly! Butter can't fly! But a butterfly can. Let's go into the garden and see if we can find one.

6 What room can you bounce around in?

A ballroom.

To bounce means "to move up and down after hitting the ground." **To bounce around** means "to move all around," usually in a very large space. **Ball** has two meanings. Normally it means "a round object that bounces"—for example, a soccer ball. A **ball** can also be a big formal party, usually with dancing, and a **ballroom** is a large room for dancing.

Jessica and Paul were one of the first couples to arrive at the school gymnasium, which had been turned into a ballroom for the night of the big dance. They had a marvelous time bouncing around the dance floor from dusk until dawn. However, everyone had a big surprise when one of the storage room doors flew open, and dozens of basketballs rolled out onto the dance floor. It was *really* a "ball room" then!

7 What helps you keep your teeth together?

Toothpaste.

Toothpaste is the substance you use when you brush your teeth. **Paste** also refers to glue, which makes things stick together.

Sally's dentist told her she has two rotten teeth that must be pulled. She can't believe it, because she uses a really good toothpaste. Now she wishes the dentist could use a different "tooth paste" to glue her teeth in her mouth!

8 How do you make a lemon drop?

Hold it and then let it go.

A **lemon drop** is a hard, lemon-flavored candy that has been popular in America for many, many years. Of course, a **lemon** is a sour fruit, and **to drop** means "to let something fall."

Jimmy was sitting beside a lemon tree eating lemon drops and watching a baseball game. All of a sudden, one of the team's star players hit a home run and the baseball came flying into Jimmy's tree. It made a lemon drop, and Jimmy had a bruise on his head for two weeks!

9 Why did the boy throw a bucket of water out the window?

He wanted to see the waterfall.

Waterfall is a compound word that refers to water falling straight down over rocks, usually from a high place. For example, Niagara Falls is a famous waterfall. The meaning of this compound word is easy to understand from the separate words that make it up: **water** and **fall**.

A: Hey, you guys, what are you doing? Why is there a bucket of water on top of the door?

B: We're waiting for John to get home. He went on a hike out to the waterfall today.

A: Ooh, boy, when he comes home, he'll see another kind of water fall!

B: Shh...I hear him coming!

10   What is a drill team?

A group of dentists who work together.

A **drill team** is a group of soldiers who practice over and over until they can march together and move their guns from side to side all at the same time, with exactly the same motions. Drill teams often perform in parades. In this context, **drill** means "to practice over and over." A **drill** is also the tool a dentist uses to make holes in teeth.

Fred and Bill were buddies in the army. They were on the same drill team, practicing their military drills side by side every morning. After they left the army, they both became dentists and continued to work together. Their clients laugh and call them their favorite "drill team."

11 Why did the truck driver drive off the edge of the cliff?

He wanted to test his air brakes.

Air brakes are the brakes on large vehicles. They use air pressure for their power.

Buses and trucks need to be cautious when going down long, steep hills. If they ride the brakes too much, the air pressure in the brake system may drop. If the air pressure gets too low, the drivers may end up with no brakes at all. Then they would really be testing their "air brakes."

Section Two

What Could It Be?

The riddles in this section all ask you to guess what something is from a description. But be careful! Many of them contain words with more than one meaning, and all of them are designed to trick you!

12 What has a fork and mouth, but cannot eat?

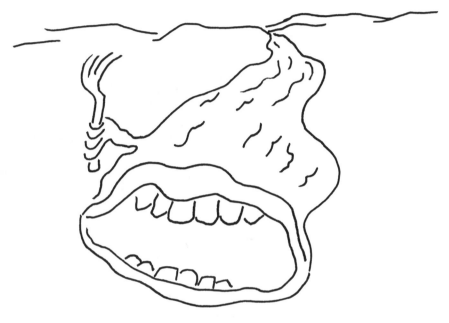

A river.

A **fork** is the pointed tool you use to carry food from your plate to your mouth. But a **fork** is also the place where a river or a road splits and goes in two different directions. The **mouth** of a river is where the river enters the ocean.

A: Look up ahead! There's a fork in the river. Which direction should we take?

B: Stay to the right. That's the side that leads down to the mouth of the river. We'll be there in about two more hours.

A: Two hours!? Let's get out of the boat then, and find a place to eat. I'm hungry, and the only mouth I care about right now is mine!

B: All you ever think about is a knife and fork...

13 What has two hands and a face, but no arms or legs?

A clock.

The **hands** and **face** are parts of the human body, of course. But the **hands** of a clock or of a watch are the two pieces of metal or plastic that point to the numbers. The **face** is the flat part that the numbers are on.

Jason has to take his alarm clock to the jeweler to be repaired. When it went off this morning, he was very sleepy, so he took it in both hands and threw it on the floor. The hands of the clock broke off, and the face was damaged. You should have seen the look on his face when he saw what he had done!

14 What can be measured, but has no length, width, or thickness?

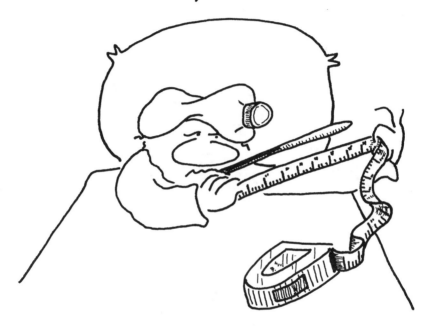

Your temperature.

To measure something is to find out how much of that thing there is, or how big the thing is. When a person is sick, the skin may become very hot. Then we say that the person has a **temperature**. Temperature is measured with a thermometer.

A: What's the matter with you? You look terrible!

B: I was upstairs measuring the bathroom for the new carpet, and suddenly I felt very weak.

A: Let me feel your forehead...Yikes, you're burning up! Let's take your temperature. That way we can measure just how sick you are.

15 What doesn't ask questions, but needs to be answered?

The telephone.

When the telephone rings, you **answer** it by picking up the receiver and saying "Hello?"

A: Would someone please answer that phone?? It's ringing off the hook!

B: OK, OK, I'll get it...Hello?...A survey? No, I don't have time to answer your questions. Sorry! [click]

16 What has a neck, but no head?

A bottle.

A person's **neck** is the part between the head and the body. The **neck** of a bottle is the long, slender part at the top. A bottle also has a lip—but no head.

Caroline was not very good as a waitress. Every time she tried to open a bottle of wine for her customers, she ended up pushing the cork down into the neck. Her boss was ready to wring her neck, he was so angry!

17 What comes down, but never goes up?

Rain.

When rain falls, we say it is **coming down**. Of course, rain can't go **up**—until it evaporates and goes back to the sky.

Tom and Karen were very disappointed. They had planned to go up in a hot air balloon this afternoon. Unfortunately, the sky got cloudy around noon, and by two o'clock the rain was coming down hard. It really was raining cats and dogs! By nighttime, the water had already gotten up over the driveway, and they couldn't even get the car out to go to the movies.

18 **What is black when it is clean and white when it is dirty?**

A blackboard.

A **blackboard** is the thing on a classroom wall that the teacher writes on when explaining something to the class. Not all blackboards are black, though. Many are green, but they're still called "blackboards." You write on a blackboard with a piece of white chalk.

Every time the teacher covered the blackboard with writing, Toshi would offer to stay after class to clean it. It was a dirty job, but somebody had to do it. The teacher was allergic to chalk dust, so she was very grateful for Toshi's help. Needless to say, Toshi was the teacher's pet!

19 What has ears, but can't hear?

Corn.

Ears are what you hear with. Corn, one of America's most popular vegetables, also has **ears**. These are long cylinders that grow on the corn plant. An ear of corn is covered with rows of yellow grains called **kernels**.

The MacDonalds live in the Midwest. They love the months of July and August, because that's when the corn ripens. They stop at the farm stands along the side of the road and buy ears of corn fresh from the field. They take it home and boil it. (Sometimes they roast it on the barbecue, too.) The whole family loves corn on the cob dipped in melted butter! I couldn't believe my ears when Mrs. MacDonald told me her husband can eat three or four ears all by himself at one meal!

20 What has teeth, but can't chew?

A comb.

Teeth are the hard white parts of your mouth that are used for chewing food. The **teeth** of a comb are the individual points that are all in a row. Gears and zippers also have teeth.

A: Joel, would you *please* get that comb out of your mouth? You're going to chip a tooth chewing on it like that! And if one of the comb's teeth breaks off, you could choke on it!

B: Mom....!

A: Here, if you have to chew on something, have a piece of sugarless gum. It's much better for your teeth. And then I want you to go brush your teeth and comb your hair. We need to leave for church in fifteen minutes.

21 What goes up and down but doesn't move?

A staircase.

Usually, when we say that something or someone **goes up** or **goes down**, we mean that it moves from one place to another by going higher or lower. However, some things that don't move—like stairs, ladders, or roads— but that are used to move in this way are also said to **go up** or **go down**.

A: Excuse me, I'm looking for the offices of Rogers and Dolinski Associates. I think they're on the second floor. Can you tell me how to get up there quickly? I'm late for a job interview.

B: Yes, ma'am. If you don't mind taking the stairs, it's a lot faster than waiting for the elevator. That door over there leads to the staircase. Take the stairs up to the second floor. When you come out the door at the top of the stairs, you'll be right across from Rogers and Dolinski Associates.

A: Great! Thanks for your help! I'm really up for this interview. Wish me well!

Section Three

Double Your Pleasure

In this section you will find more riddles in which words have more than one meaning.

22 Why did the boy put his radio in the refrigerator?

He wanted to hear cool music.

Cool has two meanings. It can mean "somewhat cold." In everyday speech, **cool** can also mean "wonderful, exciting, great."

A: Wow! What a great song!

B: You said it! This station plays really cool music. I could listen for hours.

A: Me too. Hey, tell you what, let me get us a nice, cool drink from the fridge, and we can just sit back and listen for awhile.

B: Cool! Sounds like a great idea!

23 What has four wheels and flies?

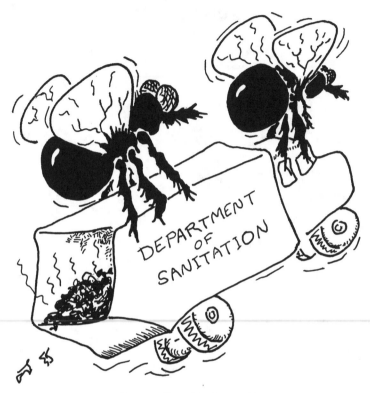

A garbage truck.

Flies is the third person singular of the verb **to fly**, which means "to move through the air." But **flies** is also the plural of the noun **fly**, which is a common household insect that you find flying around garbage or dead, rotting things.

There was a lot of excitement just outside of town today. It seems that one of the city garbage trucks was speeding. The driver couldn't stop, and the truck went flying off the road. It flew over a fence and landed in a field with all four wheels in the air. All the garbage spilled out. You've never seen so many flies in all your life!

30

24 Where was Solomon's temple?

At the side of Solomon's head.

A **temple** is a place of worship in some religions.
Solomon was a king of ancient Israel who built a famous
temple in Jerusalem. The **temple** is also the side part of
the head, just in front of and above each ear.

A: I've got a splitting headache! My temples have been hurting all
day.
B: Do you have any idea what brought it on, Dad?
A: I'm not sure. I went to the temple this morning for the early ser-
vice, so I didn't have time for breakfast.
B: That must have done it!

25 If you don't feel well, what do you probably have?

A pair of gloves on your hands.

Feel can refer to one's health or one's emotional state. For example, you can **feel well**, **feel sick**, or **feel sad**. **Feel** can also refer to your sense of touch. We **feel** things with our fingers or hands.

A: What's the matter, Garth? You're looking quite pale.
B: I don't know what's wrong, but I'm really feeling lousy.
A: Come here, let me feel your forehead and see if you have a fever.
B: I don't think I do. I may just be feeling tired.

26 What kind of coat is made without buttons and is wet when you first put it on?

A coat of paint.

A **coat** is a piece of clothing that covers your other clothes. A **coat** can also be a thin covering of some substance such as paint or dust all over a surface.

A: Wow! I like the new color you're painting the living room!
B: Thanks, but be careful. I just put on the first coat and it's still wet. Here, let me take your coat. I'll hang it up in the closet and we'll get started painting the dining room.

27 What kind of cake tastes awful?

A cake of soap.

A **cake** is a baked sweet made from flour, eggs, and other ingredients. A bar of soap can also be referred to as a **cake** of soap.

A: Hi, Jane. Where are you off to?

B: Oh, I'm going to the bakery to pick up a birthday cake for my son. How about you?

A: I'm heading for the drug store. I need a couple of cakes of soap, some baby powder, and some aspirin.

28 How do you keep a rhinoceros from charging?

CASHIER

Take away his credit cards.

To charge means "to rush at someone or something to attack it." **To charge** something also means to pay for an item by using a credit card.

A: I heard you went on a safari. How did it go?

B: Great! But we had a scare—out of nowhere, a huge tiger came charging at us. Thank heaven we were able to scare him off with rifle shots!

A: That sounds exciting. Tell me, was the trip expensive?

B: It certainly was. I had to charge the plane tickets to my credit card. It will take me months to pay off! But it was worth it.

29 What's the best way to make pants last?

Make the jacket first.

To last means "to stay in good and usable condition."
Last also describes something that comes after everything else. The final person or thing in a series is **last**.

A: I like your new suit. It looks great on you! Who's your tailor?

B: Nick Stratos, over on Main Street. Everything he makes lasts forever.

A: The last time I went to the tailor, the hem fell out of my pants the very next day.

30 How many feet are there in a yard?

It depends on how many people are standing in it.

A **foot** is a measure of distance used in the U.S. It equals about 30.48 cm. Three **feet** equal one **yard**, another distance of measure (=0.9144 meter). A **foot** is also a body part, of course, and a **yard** is also the grassy area around a house.

The Thompsons' yard measures 60 feet by 30 feet (20 yards by 10 yards). They planted a huge garden there this spring. Unfortunately, because it's such a nice big yard, all the kids from the neighborhood come to play there. With all those little feet trampling the flowers and plants, the Thompsons have a hard time keeping the yard looking nice.

31 What can you serve, but never eat?

A tennis ball.

To serve means "to put food in front of someone." **Serve** is also a term used in the game of tennis. It means "to start the game by hitting the ball to one's opponent."

A: Did you enjoy the tennis match?

B: I sure did! I was particularly impressed with how well Bettina serves. She hit the ball so hard and fast that the other player could hardly see it coming.

A: I agree. Now that the match is over, I could go for a sandwich and a drink. Do you know if they're still serving lunch in the coffee shop?

B: No, let's find someplace else to eat. The service in there is always terrible.

32 Where can you find the largest diamond in the world?

On a baseball field.

A **diamond** is a beautiful, clear stone used in jewelry, but it is also the name of the playing field in the game of baseball. A baseball **diamond** is shaped something like the stone.

Although the most perfect diamonds are mined in far-off lands, in America there are diamonds that are much bigger and more precious. Any American can tell you that these diamonds are found on a baseball field!

Section Four

Why Ask?

These riddles all have simple, perfectly logical answers—but the questions are designed to make you think that there is a more complex answer. So, keep it simple and try not to think too much, and you'll be successful.

33 Which hand should you stir soup with?

Neither. You should use a spoon!

Bet you thought this was a question of table manners!

Timmy, get your fingers out of your soup! You have better manners than that! Use your spoon to stir it! And remember to keep your other hand in your lap. That's how polite people eat.

34 If six children and two dogs were under just one umbrella, how come none of them got wet?

It wasn't raining.

How come is a very informal way of asking "why?"

A: I just saw the strangest thing at the bus stop. There were all these kids and two dogs huddled under a single umbrella!

B: Why is that so strange?

A: Well, mainly because it's not raining!

35 What's the best way to win a race?

Run faster than anyone else.

When many Americans read this riddle, they might first think of a famous saying, "Slow and steady wins the race," which is often true. However, the answer to the riddle is always true.

A: Coach, what do you think I should do if I want to win the race this Saturday?

B: Well, Angela, watch your diet this week, do your stretching exercises, and I want you to train for two hours every day.

A: And that will make me win?

B: That and running like the wind. The only real way to win a race is to get to the finish line before anyone else does.

36 What has no beginning and no end?

A circle.

This is actually an ancient riddle. It's not very funny, but it sure has stayed around for a long time!

Jacob is really depressed. He doesn't feel as though his days have a beginning or end. He just runs around in circles all the time, and doesn't think he's getting anywhere. What he needs is a goal that he can move toward, so he can get out of this vicious circle.

37 Why did the chicken cross the road?

To get to the other side.

This is probably the most famous American riddle of all time. It's particularly popular with five-year-olds who've just discovered riddles.

A: Watch out! There are a bunch of chickens running across the road up there! What do you think they're doing?

B: I don't know. Maybe a wolf or some other animal is chasing them.

A: There aren't any wolves around here. The answer may be simpler than that. Maybe they just want to get to the other side of the road!

38 Why do lions eat raw meat?

Because they can't cook.

Raw means "not cooked." Many Americans do not like meat or fish that is not cooked all the way through, and many are vegetarians because they don't like the idea of eating meat.

The Jeffersons went on a camping trip through the Southwestern desert last summer. One day they went on a hike and saw a coyote eating a rabbit it had just killed. When they cooked dinner that evening, they were very careful to make their hamburgers well-done. They had seen enough raw meat that day!

39 How can you jump off a fifty-foot ladder without getting hurt?

Jump off the bottom rung.

A fifty-foot ladder would be more than 15 meters high, but the first **rung**, or step, is only about one foot off the ground.

A: I had a real scare this morning. You know I'm having my house painted. Well, I heard a lot of noise out in the yard, so I rushed out to see what had happened. The foreman told me that one of his workers had fallen off a ladder.

B: Oh, no, that's awful! Was he hurt?

A: No...as it turns out, he had fallen from the third rung, so it was only about three feet. But he had knocked over four buckets of paint all over the grass and bushes!

40 Which football player wears the biggest helmet?

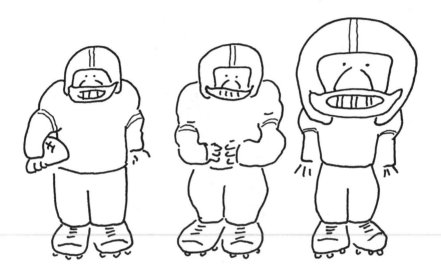

The one with the biggest head.

American football is a very aggressive sport. Players must wear helmets to protect their heads, and shoulder pads to prevent injury when they hit other players with their bodies. All the different playing positions, though, wear the same uniform.

A: Come on, guys, try on these uniforms for size. Our first game is on Saturday.

B: Coach, are there any larger helmets? This one's too small for me.

A: That's because your head is so big from thinking you're the most important player on the team, Wilson! Here, try this one.

41 Why does a firefighter wear red suspenders?

To keep his pants up.

Suspenders are pieces of elastic that men wear over their shoulders and attach to their pants to hold them up. Red is the color usually associated with firefighters.

Everyone in the firehouse was really exhausted. The alarm had sounded seven times on their shift. Every time they got back to the fire station, the alarm would go off again, and they would have to pull back on their protective pants, slip their arms through the suspenders, put on their helmets, and climb back onto the truck to go out one more time.

42 When is it bad luck to have a black cat follow you?

When you are a mouse.

According to superstition, it is bad luck for a black cat to walk across your path. This is particularly true if the cat is big enough to eat you.

Linda was having a terrible day. On her way to work, a black cat ran out into the street in front of her car. She swerved to miss it, and hit a parked car. Then everything went wrong at work. When she got home, she discovered that mice had been in her closet and had ruined some of her best clothes. She isn't superstitious, but she did wonder if that black cat had anything to do with all of this.

43 Why do we dress baby boys in blue and baby girls in pink?

Because they can't dress themselves.

The traditional color for baby boys' clothing and blankets is pale blue, and for baby girls it is pink. If you don't know what the sex of the baby will be, you can give gifts of yellow clothing, which is considered appropriate for either boys or girls.

A: Did Melissa have her baby yet?

B: Yes, she did, a little boy. She dresses him in the cutest little blue designer outfits!

A: Designer outfits! Isn't that overdoing it for a new baby?

B: Well, I'm sure if he could dress himself, he'd choose something different!

44 What kind of bushes do rabbits in California sit under when it rains?

Wet ones.

You don't need to know anything about botany to answer this riddle.

Ellen and her brother Mike were out in the park when it started to pour down rain. They ran for cover under a huge bush. They soon discovered that they were sharing this bush with a whole family of rabbits. The leaves of the bush were wet with rain, but the people and animals underneath were dry as a bone.

45 What time is it when the clock strikes thirteen?

Time to get a new clock.

Americans almost never use the 24–hour clock, except in the military. We usually specify "morning" by using **A.M.** or **in the morning** after the time, and "evening" by using **P.M.** or **in the evening** or **at night.** An American may not know what you mean if you say something is happening at "13 o'clock."

Jocelyn was trying to fall asleep last night when the grandfather clock in the hallway began to chime. ...ten, eleven, twelve, thirteen... Thirteen! She realized that the clock must be on the fritz again. If the shop couldn't fix it this time, she knew she would just have to buy a new clock. The shop opens at 10 o'clock in the morning, and Jocelyn decided she would be there as soon as they opened their doors.

Section Five

Mind Twisters

These riddles are designed to trick you. Read the questions very carefully!

46

If a rooster laid an egg on top of a pointed-roof henhouse, which side would the egg roll off?

Neither. A rooster can't lay eggs.

A rooster is a male chicken. The female is called a hen. Obviously, only the female can lay eggs.

47 There was a big alligator walking down the street with a little alligator. The little alligator was the big alligator's son, but the big alligator wasn't the little alligator's father. Who was the big alligator?

The little alligator's mother.

48 If an electric train travels ninety miles an hour in a westerly direction, and the wind is blowing from the north, in which direction will the smoke blow?

There is no smoke from an electric train.

49 Who can jump higher than a house?

Anyone! A house can't jump.

50

Two fathers and two sons went fishing. Each fisherman caught a fish, yet only three fish were caught. How is this possible?

A boy, his father, and his grandfather went fishing together.

51 At this moment, everyone in the world is doing the same thing. What is it?

Getting older.

52 If you dropped a tomato on your toe, would it hurt much?

Yes, if it were in a can.

53 How much dirt is there in a hole exactly one foot deep and one foot wide?

None. A hole is empty.

You don't need to know anything about American measurements to find the answer to this riddle!

54

Two teachers teach at the same school. One is the father of the other's son. What relation are they to each other?

Husband and wife.

55 What can you hold in your left hand, but not in your right hand?

Your right elbow.

Try it if you don't believe us!

56 Can a man living in New York be buried in California?

No! He's still living!

Section Six

How's Your Math?

These riddles all use numbers to keep you from finding the solution. Think as logically as possible!

57 A cowboy had twelve cows. All but nine died. How many cows did he have left?

Nine.

The quantity following the phrase **all but** or **all except** will always tell you how many of something are left. Usually, though, **all but** suggests that what remains is only a small part of the original number or amount!

58

Two men were playing checkers. They played five games. Each man won the same number of games. How is this possible?

They played different people.

59 How many books can you put into an empty school bag?

None. If you put a book in it, the bag is no longer empty.

60 A donkey was tied to a rope six feet long. A bale of hay was eighteen feet away, and the donkey wanted to eat the hay. How could he do it?

Easily, if the other end of the rope wasn't tied to anything.

The answer would have been different if the riddle had said the donkey was **tied *up* with** the rope, and not just **tied *to*** it. For your information, 6 feet = 1.83 meters, and 18 feet = 5.49 meters.

61 It takes twelve one-cent stamps to make a dozen. How many six-cent stamps does it take to make a dozen?

Twelve. It takes only twelve of *anything* to make a dozen.

62 If you have five potatoes and you have to divide them equally among three people, what should you do?

Mash them first.

63 If there were six crows sitting on a bench and a hunter shot one of them, how many would be left?

None. The noise of the gun would frighten the others away.

64 A girl was nine on her last birthday, and she will be eleven on her next. How is this possible?

Today is her tenth birthday.

65

If you count twenty horses on your right going into town, and twenty horses on your left coming home, how many horses have you counted in all?

Twenty. You counted the same horses coming and going.

66 If it takes three minutes to boil an egg, how long will it take to boil three eggs?

Three minutes, if they're in the same pot.

There's an old proverb, "Don't put all your eggs in one basket" (which means, "Don't risk everything you have on one solution"). Apparently this doesn't apply to pots.

67 How do you make seven even?

Take off the *s.*

Seven is an **odd** number: that is, it can't be divided by two. The opposite of an odd number is an **even** number.

Section Seven

Watch Your Language!

The language in these riddles may lead you off in the wrong direction. The wording is designed to trick you, so be ready for unexpected answers!

68 A man who worked in a butcher shop was six feet tall and wore size eleven shoes. What did he weigh?

Meat.

If people are heavy, they **weigh** a lot. We might say that they are **overweight**. However, a person can **weigh** other things by putting them on a scale.

Mr. Brown, the butcher, was a big guy who was somewhat overweight. One day, while he was weighing some steaks for one of his customers, his scale broke down and he had to weigh the meat again on another scale.

69 What is the best exercise for losing weight?

Pushing yourself away from the table.

Americans sometimes seem obsessed with exercise and losing weight. There are many ways to lose weight. One is exercise, but another is to limit what you eat.

A: Another piece of cake?

B: No, thanks. I'm trying to take off a couple of pounds.

A: Aw, come on! You can exercise to do that!

B: True. But I've found that the best way to keep off the weight is just to push myself away from the table when I'm full!

70 What's the difference between a hill and a pill?

One is hard to get up,
the other is hard to get down.

To get has lots of meanings, especially when it's followed by a preposition. **To get up a hill** means "to climb it." **To get something down** can mean, among other things, "to swallow something."

While on a camping trip, Steven realized that he was out of shape. He breathed harder and harder as he tried to get up to the top of the mountain. He tried eating a chocolate bar to give him more energy, but he was breathing so hard that he had trouble getting it down.

71 What occurs once in a minute, twice in a moment, and not once in a hundred years?

The letter m.

The answer to this riddle requires that you look at the spelling of the words, not their meanings!

A: Gosh, this crossword puzzle is hard! All the answers are words about time.

B: I'm really good at crossword puzzles.

A: OK, if you're so good, help me out. What time-word has two *m*'s and means "one thousand years"?

B: That's easy. *Millennium*.

A: Wow! You *are* good!

72 Which is better: "The house burned down" or "The house burned up"?

Neither. They're both bad!

To **burn down** is used mainly about buildings. **To burn up** means that something burns completely so that nothing is left. Either way, the outcome is bad! When talking about people, **to burn someone up** means "to make them very angry."

A: Did you see the paper this morning? The Smiths' house completely burned down yesterday.

B: Did it burn up their art collection, too? It was really valuable, I hear.

A: Yes, I'm afraid so.

B: You know, it really burns me up that we don't have better fire protection in this town! I'm going to write the city council to complain about that.

73 What is the similarity between "2 + 2 = 5" and your left hand?

Neither is right.

Right can mean "correct." In this sense, the answer to the math problem isn't **right**. **Right** is also the opposite of "left."

A: Can you give me directions to the post office?
B: Sure. Go down three blocks and turn right. Then go one block and turn left.
A: Right and then left?
B: Right!
A: Right and then *right*?
B: No, no, right and then left!

74 What can be right, but never wrong?

An angle.

Right has yet another meaning in geometry: a 90° angle.

A: If a right angle has ninety degrees, how many degrees does a left angle have?

B: I guess a left angle has ninety degrees, too.

A: Wrong! There's no such thing as a left angle!

B: Ooops, you're right! I never was very good at geometry...

75 What is it that a man can use for shaving, polishing his shoes, and sleeping in?

A razor, a brush, and a pair of pajamas.

No one said that the answer had to be one item for all three activities!

A: Look, I just bought a new, all-in-one travel kit.
B: What's in it?
A: There's a razor, a brush, and a pair of pajamas.
B: What, no traveler's checks?
A: I wish!

76 What is all over the house?

The roof.

All over usually means "everywhere in a place." **All over** can also mean "to cover completely." To complicate things, **all over** can also mean "to be finished or ended."

A: Yuck! What is this sticky stuff all over your kitchen floor?

B: It's bug spray. It's all over the house, not just in the kitchen. We found out we had termites. They came and put huge plastic sheets all over the house and sprayed everywhere. We had to leave for two days.

A: It's good that you found the termites. If you let them eat away for too long, it's all over!

77 What is a UFB?

An Unidentified Flying Banana.

The acronym **UFO** stands for "Unidentified Flying Object." This is what flying saucers and mysterious objects in the sky are called. This riddle puts a twist on this expression.

Timothy loved playing jokes. One day, he contacted the aviation authorities and told them he had seen a UFO. When asked to describe it, he told them it was long, curved, and yellow. He said it might be called a "UFB." When he told them what that was, no one thought it was funny.

78 How do you spell "mousetrap" with only three letters?

C-A-T.

Mousetraps are made to catch mice. Some are made of wood, others are made of something else. The American interest in inventing new technology is sometimes called "building a better mousetrap." There's an old saying: "Build a better mousetrap, and the world will beat a path to your door."

A: This place is infested with mice. I've set mousetraps all over the place, and I still can't get rid of them.

B: Why don't you try nature's supreme mousetrap?

A: And what would that be?

B: I'll give you a hint. It likes mice even more than it likes fish!

Section Eight

Piece of Cake

Piece of cake is an expression that means "very easy." The riddles in this chapter all contain idioms. To understand the humor, you'll need to understand the idioms.

79 Why did the piano student put her head on the piano?

Because she wanted to play by ear.

To play by ear is to play a musical instrument by remembering a tune you've heard and picking it out on the instrument without reading the music from a page.

A: Marla, where did you learn to play that tune?
B: I heard it a couple of times on the radio, and then sat down and picked it out on the piano.
A: That's marvelous! Have you ever had any formal lessons?
B: A few, but I don't read music very well. I mostly play by ear.

80 Why did the man quit his job as a garbage collector?

He was always down in the dumps.

A **dump** is the place where garbage is taken after it is collected from the houses. When people are **down in the dumps**, it means that they are sad and depressed.

A: Where's your smile, Fred? You look so down in the dumps!

B: I'm not at all happy with my job. I don't like spending all my time at the dump. I'm sick of being a garbageman.

A: Then quit your job and find something you like to do.

B: That's easy for you to say...but it is good advice.

81 Why did the teenager put his clock in the oven?

He wanted to have a hot time.

To have a hot time means "to thoroughly enjoy oneself."

A: What are you doing with that clock?

B: I'm putting it in the oven...

A: Are you crazy?

B: Just kidding! I'm getting ready for a hot time at the party tonight, and thought I'd start a little early.

82 Why did the farmer plant sugar cubes?

Because he wanted to raise Cain.

To raise Cain means "to make noise" or "to cause a lot of trouble." Cain is a character in the Bible who was one of the very first people, and was the first murderer, according to the story. **To raise** can mean both "to bring back from the dead" or "to cause to grow," among other meanings. Sugar **cane** is the plant from which sugar is made.

To celebrate the success of the sugar crop, the workers raised Cain all night long. The next morning, they were back in the fields preparing them so they could raise next year's crop of sugar cane.

83 Who has the strongest fingers in the world?

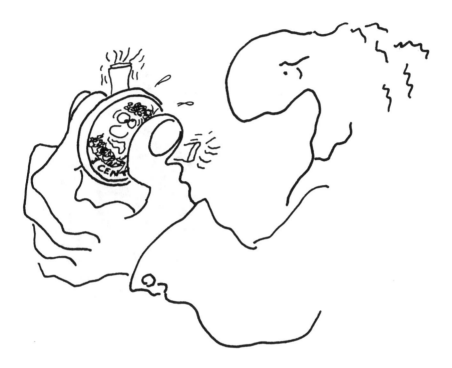

A miser, because he's always pinching pennies.

To pinch means "to squeeze tightly in one's fingers." A person who **pinches pennies**—a **penny-pincher**—is a person who does not like to spend money. Another name for this sort of person is a **miser**.

Michelle's swimming teacher told her to buy a nose plug, because she always pinches her nose before she dives in the pool. Michelle is a bit of a miser, so she was going to buy the cheapest one she could find. The teacher told her not to pinch pennies, because a cheap nose plug wouldn't work well.

84 Why was the mother flea so sad?

Because her children were going to the dogs.

A **flea** is a bloodsucking parasite that lives on dogs and cats. The expression **to go to the dogs** means "to go to ruin" or "to go with bad company."

A: Our poor dog Fido has been scratching all day. Do you think he has fleas?

B: Probably. I'll give him a bath.

A: Good idea. I'll bet he got them at the neighbors' house.

B: Yeah, their house has really gone to the dogs.

85 Why did the student always take cold baths?

Because he didn't want to get into hot water.

When people are in **hot water**, it means that they are "in a lot of trouble."

When Bill was late to meet his girlfriend, he knew he was going to be in hot water. When he got to the restaurant, she was sitting and drinking hot tea, and glaring at him very angrily.

86 When can a man be six feet tall and be short at the same time?

When he is short of money.

Six feet = 1.83 meters. The expression **to be short of** means "to not have enough of something."

A: Hey, Jack! Can you lend me a couple of bucks? I'm a little short of cash, and I'd like to take Melissa to dinner and a movie.

B: How can you be short? You just got paid! OK, here's twenty bucks. If you ask me, though, Melissa's too short for a tall guy like you.

A: Come on! Height doesn't matter! She has a heart of gold.

87 What happens to a refrigerator when you pull its plug?

It loses its cool.

The word **cool** normally means "somewhat cold." **To lose one's cool** is an expression that means "to become angry and lose control of one's feelings."

A: Why is the ice cream all melted?

B: Oh, no! I unplugged the fridge to clean behind it, and I forgot to plug it back in! It should still be cool, though.

A: Well, it's not! Look at this! Everything in the freezer is ruined!

B: Don't lose your cool! I'll go to the store and replace everything.

88 Why did the teenager put sugar under her pillow?

She wanted to have sweet dreams.

If something is **sweet**, it has a taste like that of sugar.
Sweet can also mean "nice" or "pleasant," which is what
it means in the expression **to have sweet dreams**.

If you want to have sweet dreams, you must think pleasant
thoughts. Eating a lot of candy before you go to bed will not give you
sweet dreams. It will only give you a stomachache.

89 What happened when the icicle landed on the man's head?

It knocked him cold.

An **icicle** is a long piece of ice that forms when water drips down and freezes. **To knock someone cold** means "to make someone unconscious by hitting him."

A: It has been so cold lately! Have you noticed all the icicles hanging down from the rooftops?

B: Don't talk to me about icicles! I was walking down the street and one of them broke loose from a building! It just missed me! If it had hit me, it probably would have knocked me cold!

90 Why are comedians like doctors?

They keep people in stitches.

Stitches are the pieces of thread that doctors use to hold together an incision after a surgical operation. If you make people laugh helplessly, we say that you **keep them in stitches.**

Derrick was always funny. Even at a young age he could keep people in stitches with his jokes. As an adult, however, he decided to go into medicine. As a surgeon, he could keep people in stitches—but of course, in a very different way!

Section Nine

It's Not What You Think...

The riddles in this section will lead you astray.
More often than not, the first solution that
comes to mind is **not** the solution to the riddle!
There are no clues to help you with these, so it's
all up to you.

91 What is the first thing that a gardener puts in the garden?

His foot.

92 Where is the ocean deepest?

On the bottom.

93 On what side of a school does an oak tree grow, traditionally?

On the outside.

94 Do you say "Nine and five *are* thirteen," or "Nine and five *is* thirteen"?

Neither. Nine and five is *fourteen*.

95 What is the perfect cure for dandruff?

Baldness.

96 What do you call a person who doesn't have all his fingers on one hand?

Normal.

97 What's the best thing to take when you're run over?

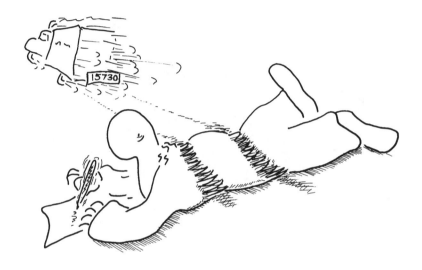

**The license plate number
of the car that hit you.**

98 How many months have twenty-eight days?

All of them.

99 Name five things that contain milk.

Ice cream, cheese...and three cows.

100 What's the best way to find a pin in a rug?

**Take off your shoes and
walk around barefoot.**

101 How many bricks does it take to finish a house?

Only one—the last one!

Index of Riddles

NOTE: Numbers refer to riddle numbers, and not to page numbers.

LANGUAGE AND REFERENCE BOOKS

Dictionaries and References
VOX Spanish and English Dictionaries
Cervantes-Walls Spanish and English Dictionary
Klett German and English Dictionary
NTC's New College French & English Dictionary
NTC's New College Greek & English Dictionary
Zanichelli New College Italian & English Dictionary
Zanichelli Super-Mini Italian & English Dictionary
NTC's Dictionary of Spanish False Cognates
NTC's Dictionary of German False Cognates
NTC's Dictionary of *Faux Amis*
NTC's American Idioms Dictionary
NTC's Dictionary of American Slang and
  Colloquial Expressions
Forbidden American English
Essential American Idioms
Contemporary American Slang
Everyday American English Dictionary
Everyday American Phrases in Content
Beginner's Dictionary of American English Usage
NTC's Dictionary of Grammar Terminology
Robin Hyman's Dictionary of Quotations
Guide to Better English Spelling
303 Dumb Spelling Mistakes
NTC's Dictionary of Literary Terms
The Writer's Handbook
Diccionario Inglés
El Diccionario Básico Norteamericano
British/American Language Dictionary
The French-Speaking World
The Spanish-Speaking World
Guide to Spanish Idioms
Guide to German Idioms
Guide to French Idioms
101 Japanese Idioms
Au courant
Guide to Correspondence in Spanish
Guide to Correspondence in French
Español para los Hispanos
Business Russian
Yes! You Can Learn a Foreign Language
Japanese in Plain English
Korean in Plain English
Easy Chinese Phrasebook and Dictionary
Japan Today!
Everything Japanese
Easy Hiragana
Easy Katakana
Easy Kana Workbook
The Wiedza Powszechna Compact Polish & English
  Dictionary

Picture Dictionaries
English; French; Spanish; German

Let's Learn...Picture Dictionaries
English, Spanish, French, German, Italian

Verb References
Complete Handbook of Spanish Verbs
Complete Handbook of Russian Verbs
Spanish Verb Drills
French Verb Drills
German Verb Drills

Grammar References
Spanish Verbs and Essentials of Grammar
Nice 'n Easy Spanish Grammar
French Verbs and Essentials of Grammar
Real French
Nice 'n Easy French Grammar
German Verbs and Essentials of Grammar
Nice 'n Easy German Grammar
Italian Verbs and Essentials of Grammar
Essentials of Russian Grammar
Essentials of English Grammar
Roots of the Russian Language
Reading and Translating Contemporary Russian
Essentials of Latin Grammar
Swedish Verbs and Essentials of Grammar

Welcome to...Books
Spain, France, Ancient Greece, Ancient Rome

Language Programs: Audio and Video
Just Listen 'n Learn: Spanish, French, Italian, German,
  Greek
Just Listen 'n Learn PLUS: Spanish, French, German
Speak French
Speak Spanish
Speak German
Practice & Improve Your...Spanish, French, Italian,
  German
Practice & Improve Your...Spanish PLUS, French PLUS,
  Italian PLUS, German PLUS
Improve Your...Spanish, French, Italian, German: The
  P & I Method
Conversational...in 7 Days: Spanish, French, German,
  Italian, Portuguese, Greek, Russian, Japanese, Thai
Everyday Japanese
Japanese for Children
Nissan's Business Japanese
Contemporary Business Japanese
Basic French Conversation
Basic Spanish Conversation
Everyday Hebrew
VideoPassport in French and Spanish
How to Pronounce Russian Correctly
How to Pronounce Spanish Correctly
How to Pronounce French Correctly
How to Pronounce Italian Correctly
How to Pronounce Japanese Correctly
L'Express: Ainsi va la France
L'Express: Aujourd'hui la France
Der Spiegel: Aktuelle Themen in der Bundesrepublik
  Deutschland
Listen and Say It Right in English
Once Upon a Time in Spanish, French, German
Let's Sing & Learn in French & Spanish

"Just Enough" Phrase Books
Chinese, Dutch, French, German, Greek, Hebrew,
  Hungarian, Italian, Japanese, Portuguese, Russian,
  Scandinavian, Serbo-Croat, Spanish
Business French, Business German, Business Spanish

Language Game and Humor Books
Easy French Vocabulary Games
Easy French Crossword Puzzles
Easy French Word Games and Puzzles
Easy French Grammar Puzzles
Easy Spanish Word Power Games
Easy Spanish Crossword Puzzles
Easy Spanish Vocabulary Puzzles
Easy French Word Games and Puzzles
Easy French Culture Games
Easy German Crossword Puzzles
Easy Italian Crossword Puzzles
Let's Learn about Series: Italy, France, Germany, Spain,
  America
Let's Learn Coloring Books in Spanish, French, German,
  Italian, English
Let's Learn...Spanish, French, German, Italian, English
  Coloring Book-Audiocassette Package
My World in...Coloring Books: Spanish, French,
  German, Italian
German à la Cartoon
Spanish à la Cartoon
French à la Cartoon
101 American English Idioms
El alfabeto
L'alphabet

Getting Started Books
Introductory language books in Spanish, French,
  German, Italian

Ticket to...Series
France, Germany, Spain, Italy (Guide and audiocassette)

Getting to Know...Series
France, Germany, Spain, Italy,
  Mexico, United States

PASSPORT BOOKS
a division of *NTC Publishing Group*
Lincolnwood, Illinois USA